J
821.914
Lev

Levin. Vadim

Silly horse.

$15.95

	DATE		

VADIM LEVIN

SILLY HORSE

ILLUSTRATED BY EVGENY ANTONENKOV

TRANSLATED FROM RUSSIAN
BY TANYA WOLFSON
AND TATIANA ZUNSHINE

PUMPKIN HOUSE

Special thanks to Carlo Scaccia, Katya Kadyshevskaya,
Neal Cantrell, Will Zink, Judy Lieber, and Laura Zakin
for their invaluable help.

Text ©1969 Vadim Levin.
Illustrations ©2005 Evgeny Antonenkov.

Translations ©2005 Tanya Wolfson: "A Little Poem About a Big Rain," "A Really Scary Midnight Tale With a Telescope," "The Tale of a Trunk," "A Sad Song About a Sweet Baby Elephant I Don't Have," "Mister Snow," "A Wintertime Lullaby About Daniel-Danny, His Dad, and His Cat," "The Tale of a Calf."

Translations ©2005 Tatiana Zunshine: "Silly Horse," "A Green Story," "Jonathan Bill," "Wicky-Wacky-Wocky Mouse," "A Puppy Story," "Billy and Mabel," "Mr. Croakley."

First Edition

Silly Horse / Vadim Levin / Evgeny Antonenkov
Summary: A translation of humorous poems first published in Russia in 1969.

ISBN 0-9646010-1-X

10 9 8 7 6 5 4 3 2 1

Book Design: Evgeny Antonenkov
Book Production: Bookwrights
Book Cover Production: Peri Poloni

Published by **Pumpkin House, Ltd**
P.O. Box 21373
Columbus, Ohio 43221-0373

Printed in China.

A LITTLE POEM ABOUT A BIG RAIN

For a month the sky's been grey.
All we get is rain all day:

Soaking houses, trees and leaves,
Dripping noses, shoes and sleeves,

Soggy ground is soaked right through,
Parks and fields are soaking too,

And too far away to see
Ships are soaking in the sea.

A GREEN STORY

Auntie Jackie
(*In a green jacket*),
Uncle Matt
(*With a green hat*),
Together with daughters Odetta and Greta
(*Each of them wearing a fuzzy green sweater*),
Went in a carriage
To the town of Rosetta
To witness the marriage
Of aunt Henrietta.
But their son Johnny on a grey dappled pony
(*Who had a green saddle and liked macaroni*)
Chased after them in the morning.

Auntie Jackie
(*In a green jacket*),
Uncle Matt
(*With a green hat*),
Together with daughters Odetta and Greta
(*Each of them wearing a fuzzy green sweater*),
Came back in the carriage
They took to Rosetta
To witness the marriage
Of aunt Henrietta.
But their son Johnny
And the grey dappled pony
(*Who had a green saddle and liked macaroni*)
Took a train on the following morning.

JONATHAN BILL

Jonathan Bill,
Who chased off the hill
A bear in southern Peru,

Jonathan Bill,
Who spent a great deal
Buying a grey kangaroo,

Jonathan Bill,
Who saved at his mill
A million bottle corks,

Jonathan Bill,
Who fed his mean bull
Dates on a silver fork,

Jonathan Bill,
Who once cured a chill
With mustard plaster and oats,

Jonathan Bill,
Who finds it a thrill
Teaching singing to goats,

Jonathan Bill,
Who sailed to Brazil
To meet his aunt Maud for lunch -

- Well!

It turns out
that Jonathan Bill
REALLY enjoyed

FRUIT PUNCH!

Preface to the scary part

What is now about to transpire
Can make the weakhearted expire.
If your brow begins to perspire
I suggest you make haste and retire.

The scary part

Mr. and Mrs. Bockley
Woke up in a state of unrest.
Mr. and Mrs. Bockley
Unlocked the family chest.
Inside they rummaged and groped
Till under the old knicknacks
They found
A telescope
And walnuts -
Four heavy sacks.

Up the winding staircases
Climbed Mr. and Mrs. Bockley.
Sweat ran down their faces,
Their knees almost buckled,
The old building shook and groaned,
The stairs twisted round and round,
But they huffed up and puffed up
Till they stood on the rooftop.

At the edge of the slanting slope,
Until the break of dawn

THEY CRACKED NUTS WITH THE TELESCOPE!

And
the shells
they threw
down
down
d
o
w
n
. . .
. .

Afterword to the scary part

Yes, but promise
You'll never throw junk
From the roof -
Folks below
Might consider it
Less than a compliment.

And another thing -
Even if the box says
"Breakproof,"

NEVER
Crack nuts
With an optical
Instrument!

SILLY HORSE

A horse has four shoes with black rubber soles,
Two of them new, but the others have holes.

If the weather is fair, no rain in the news,
The horse likes to wear her best pair of shoes.

When the first wave of snowflakes whirls in the air
She goes home to change to a worn-out pair.

When it's muddy or icy, and folks slip and slide,
The horse still goes out, but the shoes stay inside.

Silly horse, don't be concerned for a shoe!

Isn't your health more important to you?

THE TALE OF A TRUNK

A grave-looking Turkey walks next to the gully
Pushing a large iron trunk on a dolly.

He is stopped in his tracks by a baggageless Cow,
"Sir, what's in your trunk?   I am dying to know!"

"Madam, we've hardly acquainted, such manners!
Please step aside, as my trunk has sharp corners!"

But the Cow blocks his path with amazing precision
And darkly announces her final decision,

"Indeed, I must make myself perfectly clear -
Until I find out, I am staying right here!"

You'll find that the Turkey is there to this day.
The glowering Cow is still barring his way.

The trunk is still there, and the lid is still down.
The contents,
Alas,
To this day are
Unknown.

WICKY-WACKY-WOCKY
MOUSE

Wicky-Wacky-Wocky Mouse
Built himself a little house.
It has no windows,
Walls or floor,

It has no roof,
It has no door,
And yet, quite cozy is the house
Of Wicky-Wacky-Wocky Mouse.

Wicky-Wacky-Wocky Cat
Hums a ditty in B-flat.
It has no words,
But have no doubt
He knows just what
It's all about.
His tummy's feeling nice and fat,
Wicky-Wacky-Wocky Cat.

A SAD SONG ABOUT A SWEET BABY ELEPHANT I DON'T HAVE

I have many animals here in my wood:
A badger, a moose and a mole.
A partridge flies high up a tree with its brood
When foxes are out on a stroll.

A hedgehog is taking a leisurely jaunt
As beetles hide under a stone...
But a sweet baby elephant is what I want,
An elephant of my own.

The hedgehog embroiders my shirt with detail
That's really amazing to see.
The fox sweeps my room with his bushy red tail,
The bees bring me honey for tea.

The swallows above me can sing a sweet chant,
The bear is the wisest bear known...
But a sweet baby elephant is what I want,
An elephant of my own.

MISTER SNOW

"Mr. Snow, Mr. Snow,   Will you give another show?"

"Yes, indeed, one day from now."   "Thank you kindly, Mr. Snow."

A WINTERTIME LULLABY

ABOUT DANIEL-DANNY, HIS DAD, AND HIS CAT

Daniel-Danny, his cat, and his daddy
Stayed out all day
Throwing snowballs
And sledding.
When they came home
White and soaked through entirely,
Their grandma could tell who they were,
But just barely.

Daniel-Danny,
His cat
And his father
Ate six warm hot dogs
One after the other.
And then they all sat in the den
By the fire
To warm up the ears,
Paws,
Noses
And hair.

Long shadows dance on the fireplace rug.
Daniel-Danny sleeps, toasty and snug.
The cat licks her warm paw
without any sound.
The snow from dad's hat
Trickles down
To the ground.

MR. CROAKLEY

Mr. Croakley, Esquire,
Lived in Jefferson Shire,
In a barrel he slept until dawn.

Mr. Quackley, Esquire,
Had a stroll in the shire,
And since then Mr. Croakley's been gone.

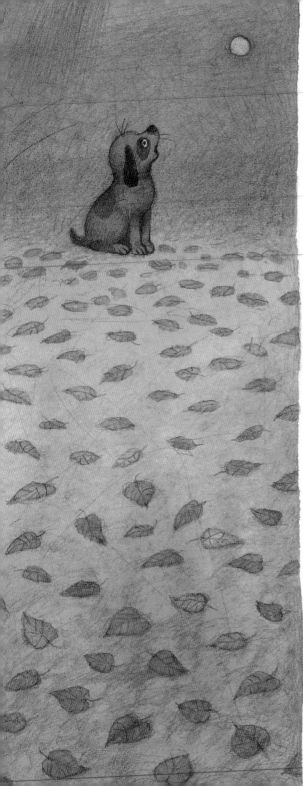

A PUPPY STORY

A puppy walked along the street,
His name was Trot (or, maybe Treat).

In blazing sun and searing heat,
The puppy walked along the street.

When the rain fell in a steady beat,
The puppy walked along the street.

And even if there was some sleet,
The puppy walked along the street.

He walked in rain,

In snow,

In fog,

And he became...

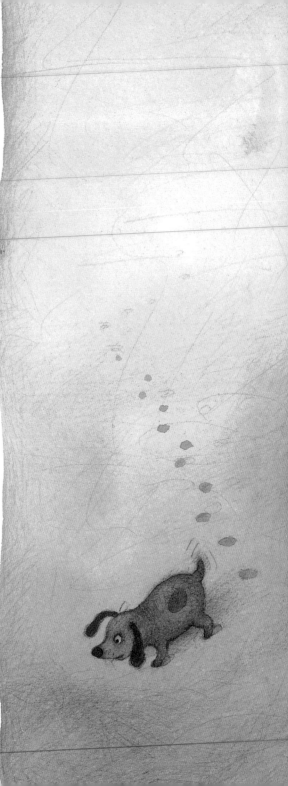

A grown-up DOG.

BILLY AND MABEL

Billy and Mabel
Climbed on the table
To meet their new Persian cat.

The first one was Bill -
He fell off with a squeal.
And Mabel fell off after that.

THE TALE OF A CALF

When I was a boy (about eight and a half)
I went to the lake every day.
And there was a funny and silly young calf
Munching on flowers or hay.

I always ran over to where he stood,
And the calf looked up and
M-o-o-o-o-ed.

He'd sniff (silly-billy) my butterfly net
Swishing his tasselled tail.
His curious nose was shiny and wet,
His ears stood up like two sails.

"I have to go home now,"
I'd tell him,
"Be good."
And the calf stood there and
M-o-o-o-o-ed.

I now own a briefcase with tables and graphs.
City life is what I chose.
But I still remember that silly young calf,
His ears and his friendly wet nose.

Has he been lonely?
How is his mood?
Did anyone laugh when he
M-o-o-o-o-ed?

Listen, if you ever go to the lake,
Keep an eye out for that calf.
His long tail will swish and the tassel will shake,
You'll look at him and you'll laugh.

Tell him I'm well
And I hope he is too.
He'll stand there and answer,

"M-o-o-o-o-o-o-o-o."